I0162646

THE
GERMINATION
*Poems and other beautiful thoughts from a
Nurtured seed*

SIZWE SITHOLE

The Germination
© Sizwe S. Sithole 2021; interior illustrations ©
Sandisa Phungula 2021
All rights reserved. No part of this book may be
used, performed or reproduced in any manner
whatsoever without written consent from the author,
except for critical articles or reviews.

Sithole, Sizwe S.
First edition 2021
ISBN: 978-0-620-96585-9

Cover design by Sizwe S. Sithole
Proofread by Noxolo Sojola
Edited by Zolile Machi, and Clement Sibanda
Interior Illustrations by Sandisa Phungula
Interior layout by Sizwe S. Sithole

Self-Published by Sizwe S. Sithole at Amazon KDP
South Africa
To contact the author,
mailto:sitholesizwewrites@gmail.com

To the hands that tenderly ploughed this field of my mind,
shovelling and digging beyond the crust of my skull
to make my cerebral a fertile ground.
To the strong hands of my Grandmother, MaNtombela.
I thank you for the deep education,
your hands laid the early foundation.
I'm yet to find words to paint your portrait in a poem
but this is my true dedication.

THE GERMINATION

The Germination

Part I

Part II

Part III

Foreword

The first Writer I ever resonated deeply with growing up was Pierre Alex Jeanty, his work felt like the unsung truth captured in bittersweet ways. It was the first time I ever read a poetry book and saw myself through the eyes of a stranger. That is until I read this masterpiece, The Germination.

Writing is hard, even for Authors who do it all the time. I resonated so deeply with how the writer went through moments where writing was almost non-existent. How, even when he had let go of poetry; poetry never let go him, as it was always calling on him. I don't know how many times I have let writing moments pass me by because I just couldn't get the words across or had some kind of writer's block, which can turn into a dark residence on its own. Definitely a Writer's nightmare. As the title of the book breathes, it has also bolstered the gift in me, making me more eager to pursue my own writing again with a fervent spirit.

The Author comes from a rich lineage of inspirational people and I have had the honour of getting to know him through this work. During this time, I have been impressed by his great humility yet singular determination to fulfill his God-given purpose to pursue black excellence and spread a message of hope and awakening. In the book there's a poem titled 'A Prayer for Spiritual Discernment' and there's a stanza that stood out for me in a significant way as it reminded me to take a deeper look within myself and the blind spots that I sometimes overlook so faithfully:

Help us Lord to not only discern
the signs of the end times;
But to also discern the signs
of the cold love inside us.
Help us discern our injustice,
indifference, and hypocrisy,
Even though we proclaimed your love
yet failed to exemplify it in practical theology.
Help us discern that church hurt is real,
and many couldn't even access a chance to heal;
even though this place was meant to be
an institution of Grace.

It is this sense of calling and predestination that seals this book. Years of poetic dormancy have led him to write this book to inspire, encourage, motivate and build faith. As the Author has so eloquently put this in his preface, *"The germination of any seed is a critical stage, for now the seed is exposed as it seeks its fullest growth in "becoming". The germination is neither the fruit, the harvest, nor the blossom of a flower that can be pollinated; it is the genesis, a precious moment whereby we celebrate the sprouting of the seed itself. The joy of germination is the seed."*

It is against this backdrop that I believe that we as Writers and Poets are timeless vessels that can penetrate people's mindsets and provoke reformation in thinking patterns. We are the nameless heroes, with poetic powers that can help our society be better.

It is my great honour and privilege to provide the foreword to this book by an incredibly talented young Writer and Poet Sizwe Sithole, the first of what I trust will be will be of many. This is an amazing book and your life will be absolutely transformed once you implement the principles it teaches. My prayer is that as you read it you will be inspired to seek and fulfill your God-given purpose and destiny, even when life's challenges appear overwhelming.

May God bless you and continue to nourish your mind and soul in reading.

Ndo The Poet
Author of: *My Black Colorful Book, and A*
Sublime Vision of Love
October 2021

Preface

"Hi, my first name is Success!
I'm a black man with the black label of Africa;
Born in the North, raised in South.
My father is a Zulu, my mother is a Xhosa;
That's a great combination,
For the future definition!"

Those were the opening lines of a poem that was titled "Let Your True Colour Show," that I had written for a Poetry Week back in high school to celebrate the beauty of my African heritage. That poem became my first true taste of the beauty of writing and the experience of performing. Reciting the poem on stage was a breath taking experience that was adorned with ecstatic noise from peers and seasoned with expressions of pride from my Teachers. I remember it like it was yesterday; it felt like poetry had publicly acknowledged me as a soul mate and gave me my very first kiss. The positive reaction gave me the affirmation that fuelled my writing passion. This was back in 2012 when I was doing Grade 10 at Luthayi High School. But my journey as a writer did not start here...

I was born on the 26th of March, 1996 in Johannesburg where I lived with my mother, Monica Mputa and I was her only child. I also stayed with my maternal Grandmother, Uncles and Aunts who had sprung from the roots of the family tree in a rural town called Dutywa in the Eastern

Cape. In 2004 I went to stay with my paternal side of the family in a township called Hammarsdale in KwaZulu-Natal and this is where I was brewed, this is where I was bred, in the house of my grandmother, Busisiwe "MaNtombela" Sithole.

My father, Siphiwe Patrick Sithole, had 5 children and I was his third born child. All my siblings lived with their mothers except my older sister Thobile Sithole, whom I went to live with in Hammarsdale when I was 8 years old and she was already in high school. When I started my second grade in 2004 at Khalawemuke Junior Primary school, I struggled with reading and writing in isiZulu because the language I had suckled as a baby from my mother was isiXhosa. Although I was very good at speaking English due to early exposure when I was living with my mother, I had no formal grasp of the English alphabet in terms of writing. I began as a slow learner in Junior Primary and it took the robust extra classes of language skills at home that my grandmother had arranged and strongly insisted that I take daily under the tutorship of my sister for me to be a competent learner.

Due to the dedicated efforts of cultivation I received at home, I became a fast improving learner and I passed all my grades in junior primary. In 2006, when I was doing grade 4, I had become so confident in writing that I developed a hobby of writing for myself. I had a nice, small exercise book that became an art accessory from my stationary that I decided to scribble songs in. I was already falling in love with rap music and listening to artists such as Zola 7, ProVerb, and H2O. Maybe that's where it all started.

Perhaps it started just a few days before Mother's Day when I was doing grade 5 at Halala senior primary in 2007. Let me first mention that back then it was disrespectful to know the teacher's full names, and our teachers really did a good job in concealing them almost as if they were secret agents. The commandment, "Thou shalt not take the teacher's name in vain" was written in our hearts and to some extent a simple "sir" or "ma'am" was enough to address them. Hence, up to this day I still know all my primary school teachers by their surnames only.

My English teacher at that time was Ms Buthelezi and she had asked the class to write a special poem dedicated to our mothers. Although I had not yet discovered the poet in me, I was really excited about the challenge and I scribbled my poem, about half a page long. I remember reading my poem to the class, I remember the silence, I remember the applause from my peers and the affirmation I received from Ms Buthelezi on that day. Ms Buthelezi will always have a special place in my heart because she saw that gold factor in me and made me believe I had potential to be and to do more.

Perhaps it really started with my English teacher in Grade 7, Mr Ngcobo. Another truly inspiring figure who made me open my first ever library card at Mpumalanga Library and wonderfully introduced me to the world I still enjoy today, the world of books, reading, and art. He always insisted that I read at least two good novels in every month. But then again, perhaps it started with a love poem that I wrote in Grade 7 for this girl in my class who had awakened the hopeless romantic in me; but I really did not know how to verbalize what I felt but what I could not mould with my mouth, I could mould with a pen and all I did was to compose my confession and imprint it on a love poem; a poem that formed my first share in the story of teenage love.

It may also have started when I got lost in the pages of "In the Ribbon of Rhythm" by Lebo Mashile or when I read "Love Child" by Gcina Mhlophe; I read those books with deep appreciation and wonder by the time I was doing grade 9 at Luthayi High School in 2011.

Grade 10 to grade 11, year 2012 and 2013 were some of my best years in my journey of writing as a Poet. Those years gave birth to a collection of poems I had titled, "The Universal Truth" that filled my 2 quire exercise book. My seed was very promising in those years, it had been so well nurtured. Through my performances at the school assembly, I rightfully certified my credentials as a poet at Luthayi High School.

Paint artists often seek inspiration from the world that surrounds them in order for their imagination to portray an artistic commentary of that world on canvas, and sometimes inspiration comes from the world within them. Poets are paint artists trapped in words; I started writing poetry because I was inspired and as that inspiration flowed, I wrote to inspire.

However, when I was doing grade 12 in 2014 at Luthayi High School, I'm not quite sure what happened to me but I just stopped writing. At first, I thought maybe this was some break or pause just to focus on completing my matric but that pause had a great extension after matric, at some point it felt like the seed in me had totally died and decayed. I honestly did not feel inspired to write anymore, and maybe this is what they call the "writer's block". Year 2015 and 2016 were years of complete silence. I recall listening to "The Dock of the Bay" song by Otis Redding; I was battling stress and some form of depression because I had failed twice to get a firm offer of acceptance for University despite a Bachelor pass in Matric. I had all the time needed to write but I had no drop of inspiration to compose even a single line.

In 2017, I finally got a firm offer to study at Mangosuthu University of Technology (MUT). As far as poetry is concerned, I only wrote a few bits here and there when I truly felt moved by something, this was the trend until 2019. I'd say those were just the "dormant" years for me and my writing. I was not even involved in poetry on campus, even when I saw some posters for poetry shows I did not pay enough attention. This is not to say I had lost direction in life, quite frankly I was flourishing in other spheres of my life, but something kept reminding me of my first love. I wouldn't say I didn't let go of poetry but I believe poetry never let go of me. Even through those silent years, I could feel its lingering presence in my mind.

2020 came and the order of the world as we know it was turned into chaos as the coronavirus pandemic ravaged both life and business. As much as this was a tragic year on so many personal levels through grief and pain, for me 2020 was also a year of collateral beauty and the lockdown turned out to be a pure gift that awakened the poet in me. Being trapped in the house actually liberated the flow of ink and the beauty to be revisited by inspiration once again. I found myself writing again and I wasn't forcing it, it just came organically. But it was deeper than just rediscovering that creative space, as a poet I felt like I had a social mandate to fulfill; a social mandate of spreading hope. Something imaginative and true really germinated during that period.

By the end of 2020 when I assembled all the pieces together, there were surprisingly not as many as I initially thought but they were definitely some of the best pieces I have ever written as a writer and I wanted to share them with people. A random idea came to me around December 2020 and the idea was to simply release the poems to the public as some "literary mixtape" by just compiling the whole thing and creating a link for anyone to freely download it, especially for my Facebook friends. But after considering the counsel of a few close friends, this is where I finally landed, in the long adventurous journey of self-publishing my first ever poetry book!

This is The Germination because after so many years of poetic dormancy, the seed of art has finally germinated into this collection of poems that I am now sharing with the whole world. It is important to note that the germination of any seed is a critical stage, for now the seed is exposed as it seeks its fullest growth in "becoming". The germination is neither the fruit, the harvest, nor the blossom of a flower that can be pollinated; it is the genesis, a precious moment whereby we celebrate the sprouting of the seed itself. The joy of germination is the seed.

My plan was to release The Germination just before Christmas in 2020 but God had other plans which were far better than mine, plans that required a certain level of discipline and patience. As you can already see in the timeline, what was initially set to be published in December 2020 has now been published in the summer of 2021. During this period, more wonderful poems were written and got the chance to be part of this book. Although the delay was unanticipated but it proved to be something that was essential; because what would have been a premature delivery then, has now reached the fullnness of time. Germination can be translated to *"ukuhluma"* in Zulu/Xhosa, this term acknowledges the beauty of a sprouting seed.

This book is a collection of poems, commentary, and personal reflections organized into four parts:

Part I explores the themes of death, grief, and hope. Part II explores the themes of politics, blackness, gender based violence and social justice. Part III explores the themes of love, life, and beauty. Part IV is an extension of part III and foreshadow of Part V. Part V is the seal of the work, it is the proclamation of faith, hope, and agape love.

Sizwe S. Sithole
Hammarsdale, Mpumalanga Township
August 2021

PART I

This is the Place

I was only 9 years old when I first heard
"Ndawo Yami" by Zamajobe.
So young yet already captured by the magic
and my little soul already longing for the mystery.
The human race has wild dreams
and it is one's duty to fulfill the chase.

Spiritually determined
like Santiago in the *O Alquimista*;
A traveling young man
with a mind open to the beauty of wonder.
My heart was seeking a place.

The world is a territory of darkness
plotted with plenty of snares,
To navigate the way, I treasured the compass
given by the Ancient of Days.
Armed with His word
 as a lamp to my feet and light to my path;
my sense of vision became clearer
as I travelled the Earth.

To my surprise,
I found myself lost in the world of words
and had my very first blind date with poetry
when I held the pen.
This was all God's plan;
my heart had found a place.

So here's a sample of my heart

and a piece of my soul in your hands.
Come inside and dine with me:
 a cry, a smile, a dance.
I hope you enjoy the view
and the interior reflections.

If you get lost in any of the corridors of thought,
I will always be there to find you.
I hope you can call this place a home.
Feel free, feel safe; this is the place.

Blessed Reassurance

Every storm has an intrinsic weakness;
A debilitating illness that decays it from within.
The winds too, no matter how strong they seem,
Their inner muscles are bound to weaken
And to die a natural death.

We know that all storms come to an end
But what we fear is the lingering destruction
they live behind.
We fear not the initiation of the storm,
But the duration of its course;
The terrifying thought
of the shipwreck it can cause.

Why is your spirit troubled when Jesus is on board?
The storm shall surely pass;
Failing to deplete the provisions of His grace,
We are not alone in this place.

The grass withers, the flower fades
But the word of our God forever reigns.
Strengthen your heart with a dose of faith,
With Christ, life does not end
in the night of the storm.

Noah lived 350 years after the Great Flood.
And even had time to plant and harvest a vineyard.
There is life after the storm
for those that teach the soul to lean on God.

In the midst of the flood, may you discern the pillar
of His word.

Before the storm, God is with us.
During the storm, God is with us.
After the storm, God is with us.
The constant friend, neither death
nor life can separate us.

So we keep sailing
Because His boundless goodness is never failing.
Here we will stand,
Within the ark of His word.

No matter how long the night may endure,
Nothing will cancel the promises
of the morning dawn.
No matter the forecasts of perilous times,
Nothing could ever outcast us
from the depth of His infinite love.

Seven Mountains of Life

Life is a road trip,
It unfolds as one departs the station
of a mother's womb.
When you look back at the Messiah's
journey to Calvary,
You untangle the web and discover a map;
One of seven mountains every man must face.

First, the Mountain of Beatitudes;
Blessings are neatly pronounced,
your journey is well defined.
For a while, it seems like the whole world approves.
Your life's ministry brings healing to everyone;
no blemishes.
But this is just the beginning of the chronicles.

Then comes the Mountain of Temptation;
Flamboyant Empires are promised
in exchange of your soul,
Your character is tested to weigh
your commitment to the high call.
The decisions you take here are very critical;
Focus and discipline are essential.

The Mount of Transfiguration comes
and sweet communion is felt,
Your face beams with glorious light
as these are the better days,
and nothing seems to trouble your way.
You are surrounded by the people who love you;

goodness and mercy overflow on your table.

Then follows the Mount of Olives.
A juxtaposition of previous mountains.
The world sits on your shoulders
and darkness seems to prevail.
Those who were once close,
seem to be the most distant.

Mountain of Golgotha comes;
an emotionally dark place
that confronts you with paralyzing questions;
where are your brothers? Where is your God?
Your mental space is dark
and you are there all alone.

But faith will carry you
beyond the suffering, humiliation
and the crucifixion of your vision.
At the Mountain of Ascension
dreams and hopes have been resurrected.
The faithfulness of the Lord is the declaration.

Finally, Mount of Zion.
A symbol of heroic courage and triumph,
a crown of honour, that you stood in the faith
though everything in the past
seemed to have been crumbling down.

The Topography of Grief

Grief is like an elongated depression,
between two rugged mountains
of hopelessness and fear.
In this valley of grief,
any curve may reveal an entirely
new landscape and direction

But sometimes you may encounter
exactly the same landmarks
you thought you had already left behind.
Try to keep going nonetheless,
do not despair; you are not forsaken.

The thick fog of shock and denial may be the first
welcome to the new reality.
Although we are mortal beings by nature,
nothing still feels so unnatural
like embracing the cold arms of death.

Soon we find ourselves exposed
to the bare rocks of pain
tumbling down before our path
and we start condemning ourselves
to the shadows of guilt.
Blaming ourselves for the things
we had no power to control.

In this landscape of grief you will also find
 the cliffs of anger and bargaining.
We become like broken glass;

cutting anyone who dares to pick up
the fragmented pieces of ourselves.

Conversations with God
and conversations with death,
bargaining for some form of life exchange.

But the path is not linear.
The trail of emotions is complex
and there is no time frame for the duration
of each bend taken.
Sometimes the lonely slopes of depression come
before the pastures of acceptance.
Irregularities are common.

Some days you feel like all the oxygen is yours
and on some days it feels like
all the valley frost has covered your lungs.
Be sure not to miss the endless stream of hope
that cuts through it.

Remember, grieving would be utterly impossible
if life did not dwell so abundantly inside you.
Remember, though the valley is a cold place,
the Spring flowers and Lilies also grow there.

Christmas Mourning

The pain hits different
when a day that used to be filled
with tremendous joy suddenly becomes a day
that reminds you of how much you have lost.

The jingles and carols sound gloomy.
The glitters and decors seem spooky.
The world was never a perfect place
but at least one could handle
the comedy-drama of life.

One night you go to bed as usual
and find yourself waking up to
an apocalyptic horror the next morning.

Death is the Grinch that has slayed
the Christmas spirit,
now the urn of my soul holds the cremated joy.
I struggle to assemble
the memory of us in those last moments
without scattering pieces of myself in the process.

Does Jesus care?
The room is filled with eloquent silence.
Where is He in the midst of all this dimness?
I try to avoid these questions
but the void within magnifies bold punctuations.

The little ones don't understand
why you never came back

from the trip to the hospital
and my heart is too shattered to communicate
the language of the coffin.

Today I refuse to take family pictures,
this fractured countenance
will not be documented in photographic raptures.
I would be lying
if I said this pain is not suffocating.
I would be lying
if I said I'm not internally drowning.

They say time heals all wounds
yet every tick feels like torture.
I ask myself, what balm of the soul
lies in the hands of a distant future?

In the midst of this unending tunnel,
something begins to gently dawn within,
something like the hymn of Horatio Spafford,
I drag my tattered voice to say,
'it is well with my soul,'
where my mind fails,
I trust the Lord's strength shall prevail.

<u>Grace Sufficient</u>

These days I'm learning how to breathe;
I'm learning how to meditate
through the pace of my lungs.
I'm learning that breathing is more
than just a respiratory exchange of gases,
more than just the contraction
and expansion of intercostal muscles.
I am learning to exhale my anxiety
and inhale enough portion of tranquillity.

Some days I feel peace like
the soothing *petrichor* of the Earth
and on other days it feels like
the thundering heart palpitations become worse.
Some days there's a mental breeze
like the ocean waves kissing the soft sands
and on other days there's a mental rock 'n' roll,
like a head wrapped in a tight band.

Anxiety is unfair.
It exaggerates emotions without your will
but I have noted something
that embarrasses anxiety when it invades,
I simply recognize it,
and give it a friendly welcome,
"Hey there, I see it's you again,
how can I help you today?"
I'm learning to talk about these visitations openly.

Do not mistaken this kindness for weakness,

It is a privilege to carry this strength.
I used to breathe through the nose
 now I have learnt to breathe through the mind
and embrace calmness.

I will recite the prayers of the psalms
and in the night I will sing my poetry like hymns.
I will write until anxiety is no more.
I will forsake no joy in the present
even if it may feel like a constant thorn in the flesh,
I will confidently rest in this: His grace is sufficient.

Ithemba

"Ithemba alibulali"
Hope never harms, it never kills.
Hope never takes away, it always gives
as long as you stay in the room filled with hope,
you're in a safe house.

Hope gives life when everything else seems lifeless.
Hope gives taste when everything is tasteless.
Hope gives life a cheerful colour
during those dusky days.
Hope is a corridor that leads to light.
Hope will not kill you
because its essence is to inspire life within you.

"Hlala ethembeni"
Reside in hope.
Several dark forces will try to shake you away
and seek to move you out from hope
but remaining has to be
your own conscious decision.

Choose hope.
If you remain, hope will nourish you,
hope will cover you
until the raging storm subsides.

Dwell in hope,
you can stay for as long as you need to
hope will always welcome you.
Hope will never ever get tired of keeping you

and hope always offers a better promise
than the present.
Hope is a strong belief that everything will
eventually be okay.

"Ungalilahl' ithemba"
Hope never forsakes us but we forsake it.
Hope will not let us go
but we are prone to let go of it.
Hope is a life partner, faithful to the vow
to be with you through thick and thin
when everyone has left,
hope stays, it says " I am here still…"
Hope has no intentions to exit your life.

No matter how thick the layers of darkness,
no matter how uncertain the future,
no matter how high the mountain or heavy the load
hope will always be here.

Hope whispers softly,
if you listen carefully, pay attention,
that small voice beats the loudest voices of despair.
Do not forsake hope,
for hope will never forsake you.

Cheerful Medicine

IsiZulu sithi "Kuhlekwa noma kufiwe."
Our forefathers understood the kind of sanity
that life insists,
as if they were saying,
if you take life's problems too seriously,
you will go insane.

When life gives us a bowl of bitter herbs,
laughter is the perfect salad dressing,
so we don't choke from the hurt.
In any depth of pain or sorrow,
laughter is never utterly banished from the soul.

The Holy Writ says, "A cheerful heart is good
medicine but a broken spirit crushes the bones."
We thank the Lord for the friends
who cultivate those endorphins;
who help us feel that gentle wind
of hope as it blows.

Suddenly hope awakens inside
despite the fixed state of the situation
but the perception has been adjusted
with a touch of God's perspective.

I believe when God gave mankind
the gift of humour,
He meant to give us an innate copying mechanism
so we can make it through the everyday
stressors of life and bitter metabolism.

A good sense of humour
is not just an accessory of good times
but an antidote of despair
under turbulent winds.

Germination

Hope is a fertilizer of the soul,
cultivating the heart
and nourishing dreams to grow.
The cords of life vibrate
to the rhythm of God's drum,
nothing is a random chance in this universe.
See the delicate balance
in your fine-tuned existence;
woven and tailored for such a time and era
because God plays no snake
and ladders and makes no errors.

Before the first motion of your mother's womb,
God sowed the first seed.
Before the first growth of your first limbs,
God already sampled the first fruit.
You were predestined to bloom.
Never desert the dormant seed of your dream
at the appointed time it will rise
and become what it should be.

Plough the field of your mind.
Remove the weeds of every doubt.
Water it with faith and nourish it with sunshine.
Pray for the farmer's patience,
In the process, note this agricultural science;
The seed dies before it truly lives.
Sometimes things have to fall apart
before they finally fall into place.

The edge to give up will come,
"Will the time to flourish ever come?" You ask.
Remember that God's blessings arrive just on time.
Our timelines and deadlines are corroded by time
and soon become irrelevant,
but God's plan and wisdom always resonates.
When the world says it's too late;
God says, be still
and watch this true seed germinate.

Part II

Imagined Realities of a Rainbow Nation

I have always admired
the magical display of a rainbow.
When I was kid, I used to stretch my mind
trying to figure out the source
and destination of this beauty as it travelled afar,
sprinkling curved colourful stripes in the sky;
a pure semblance of serenity after the rain.

As I grew older,
I observed its lessons and became wiser.
I invite you today, to take note of these proverbs
that the rainbow taught me about
humanity and nationhood.
Especially for the nation that has been hit so hard
by storms of inequality and oppression,
floods of poverty and injustice.

The colours of the rainbow share equally
no colour seeks to be more dominant than the others
each gracefully takes up its own space,
yet leaving just enough for the rest to shine.
No colour seeks to dominate
the entire sky for its own self.

The rainbow colours embrace diversity
as if they knew their beauty is in the unity.
No colour is discriminated
for its nature of birth in the sky.
No colour is segregated or relegated to inferiority.

All colours fellowship as one
in the rhythm of harmony.

In this multi-chromatic arc,
all colours run their course and flourish as they like.
From one point to another,
all have equally fair chances to exhibit themselves
in the gallery of the sky.
A rainbow is God's own poetry.
I imagine a nation that can recite it well,
I imagine a nation that can do justice
to this divine poetic piece.

Rainbows may appear as some romantic fantasy
or something you'd read about
in a novel of mystical creatures.
But rainbows are not a sci-fi fiction or fairy-tales.
Rainbows are not unicorns.
Rainbows are real.
As real as your flesh and blood.
As true as your soul.

I imagine a nation where the rainbow spirit
is not a lofty ideal
or some farfetched reality
but a reality we embrace right now,
an experience we breathe and walk in.

Like the rainbow colours,
let's share our vibrant stories
and boldly adorn the endless skies of our Nation.
Our colours shall never fade,
walking together, holding hands;
In the colourfulness of our humanity, we are one.

Black History Reimagined: Lessons from Moana of Motunui

The aim of black history should not only be to teach about the injustices and pains of the past but to also empower and impart the essence of Marcus Garvey's words: "The black skin is not a badge of shame, but rather a glorious symbol of national greatness."

There is something beautiful I learned from the Disney movie: Moana of Motunui. This destined to be Chief daughter living in some paradise Island was raised to fear the ocean and never dare swim beyond the ocean reef (because of some bad experiences that her father had with the waves). But the beautiful island was falling apart and the key to restore its beauty lay beyond the reef, beyond the boundaries of fear set by her father and Moana knew the people needed saving.

The empowerment of the story begins when Moana's grandmother relates to her a significant part of family history that Moana was never told. As she learns the true history of her heritage from all the great canoes that were hidden in the Island, Moana then discovers that her ancestors were actually the voyagers! They never stayed "within the reef" timid of the deep waters but they mastered and conquered the ocean and pioneered the discovery of Islands in generations past. This crucial backdrop of history then empowers Moana with a new perspective, not just to bask in the glories of the past but to face her present challenges with confidence and ignites her to fulfil her destiny. This spoke to me of the importance of knowing stories of courage and heroism in one's family history. Often we magnify generational curses; yes, it's important to know the demons that waged war against your family's prosperity. But it is also equally important to know the stories of those who tried to cut different curves and perhaps the original posture of your heritage before there was even any generational curse. The stories of the "voyagers" who conquered the oceans.

Even the Messiah himself came from a thick background of generational curses. Humanly speaking, he came to end the generational curse of his chief ancestor, Adam. In his genealogy there are also those who perpetuated the curses but there were also those who carried some light, such as Enoch, Boaz, David, Josiah etc. I believe that in his childhood their stories had to be related to him too, probably this godly line also inspired the courageous pursuit of his ultimate mission. This is true for my black history as well, it should not only convey the pain and grief of the ages but it should also convey the stories of excellence and triumph of my forefathers. In the historical pages of black history, there are also plenty of chapters where one can draw inspiration. Not just to bask in the glories of the past but to ignite and affirm whatever daring hope there is inside to solve the challenges of the present and have a bold conversation with the future.

Now coming to the broader context of my beloved country, South Africa. In 2019, Helen Zille made some shocking comments when she publicly tweeted that the legacy of colonialism was not all negative. In the early beginning of 2020 we also saw F.W. De Klerk publicly denying that apartheid was a crime against humanity.

This to me sparked three things: (1) perhaps these were the symptoms that revealed the regressive belief concerning our agonising chapters of history, which is held together by some portion of white citizens in South Africa. This lack of historical conviction may explain why there is little or weak repentance, tensions in our democracy and false reconciliation in our South African society. (2) If these are the distorted ideas carried by some white parents then I'm wondering what is the home schooling curriculum they teach their kids, does it convey or display any conscience and thoughtfulness at all for the past and present black experiences in this country? Could we possibly have more reckless statements about colonialism and apartheid that will be carelessly uttered in the future by their grandchildren? (3) What is the role of black history education in building a healthy and true Rainbow Nation?

Ignoring these uncomfortable conversations makes us an unhealthy society therefore we should keep engaging and confronting these wounds until we actualize the healing. Hence, I believe that the curriculum of the History subject in White/Afrikaans schools should be customized and uniquely adapted to undo the miseducation of the apartheid regime which imposed a false superiority complex on some white people in this country. Black history as related to White pupils should strive to teach why the acts of their colonial forefathers were wicked and why apartheid was a crime against humanity. Black history should lead in helping students understand the cost of true reconciliation and the kind of social conviction, transformation and policy implementation that is needed to fulfill it.

We need to get to the point where leaners have seriously intrusive and transformative dialogues. Where leaners are free and honest enough to talk about the preservation of white privilege. We need reformers of education. Of course, there are also some black pupils in these schools and that is not necessarily a hindrance but an even better opportunity to enhance and energize the life of the class discussions. I think racism, in all its forms strives in our country because our schools are weak.

True education has the power to disrupt and reverse the patterns of false education. Any "Diversity and Inclusivity Training Programs" that occur in large corporations as a result of racial prejudice are a mere reflection of this weak education. Racism is a doctrine that is bred at home. Anti-racism can be taught at schools through a genuine confrontation of white supremacy and a brave and honest reflection upon black history and social experiences of black people; the work of Dr Jane Elliot in the U.S. is an exceptional example. What does anti-racism mean to a white man? It means he not only treats his fellow black mankind with equal respect, honour, and dignity but he also possesses that mental attitude which gets revolted and protests at the sight of the slightest hint of racism from his fellow white neighbour. This is not a white man fighting for the black man; it's white man fighting for the substance of his own humanity. I write this not from hate or any form of black supremacy but from a place of genuine love constantly bothered by the fatigue of living in a false construct of a Rainbow Nation.

For the pupils in black schools however, in the hearts of townships and rural areas. We know our experiences and we know the struggle of our ancestors, the objectives of our black history should be to tell stories of black heroic courage and achievements of excellence to solve our inferiority complex. Our History should empower us. In such a persisting drought of political role models in our time, there's plenty of black virtuous leaders in the national, continental, and global history. There's so much to feast on and so much to discover far beyond the over-iconization of Nelson Mandela. There's history for black art, black jazz, black inventions and innovations etc. I find it absurd that the approach and curriculum structure of the History subject in townships/rurals should be the same as in White/Afrikaans schools in suburbs; as if these learners from such contrasting backgrounds have the same miseducation to unlearn. As if the legacy of apartheid is affecting us the same way.

Black history as related to the black child should strive to remove the psychological badge of shame and impart the sense of what Maverick said to his daughter Starr, "Being black is an honour." We do not only come from a place of pain, we come from a place of excellence. Tell the black child more about it!

Nobel Disturbance Prize

If peace is defined by the Ts & Cs of the oppressor,
peace is a deception.
If peace is a social bribery to not address inequality
and correct injustices,
peace is an illusion.
If peace is a broken harmony
when the oppressed sing,
peace is an incarceration.

Peace is not for the cowards.
The price of peace is self-denial.
Unless we are willing to disturb
and shake the feeble ideas of peace,
we will always design its symbols
and never truly attain its reality.

State of the Nation Redress

Sell us dreams no more.
The dreams in the past
still stand in the midst, unfulfilled.
Our currency of hope
can no longer partake in empty trades.
Hani, Sobukwe, and Biko
are turning in their graves.
The black man's burden
still accumulating on his shoulders.

Like a child on the 25th of December
hoping for some new shoes and clothes.
The 27th of April is commemorated
as the birth of democracy
but like Shakur, I see no changes;
what's the mandate of the constitution?
A democracy so young has sinned and grown old,
it cries for redemption.

27 years of freedom one would anticipate
some radical policy and change.
But same old shoes, same old clothes,
and history repeats itself.
Economic freedom is just a stroke of a discussion.
Land is still an unresolved question.
Free education and inertia
still asphyxiating the youth in the gutters.

Maybe it's time we change the political market.
The President will buy. We will sell.

We don't want him in Western attire,
we want him in the true regalia
of the townships and villages.
We don't want a manifesto,
we want a manifestation.
We don't want same old promising
inaugural sermons,
Mr President, that pulpit has collapsed.
Go to the lands of the landless,
The true congregation in the shacks
and preach with the integrity of your hands.

Take the Pulpit to the excluded society
but don't forget,
you are now ministering to the generation of
sceptical believers,
those of us who have been failed by the system.
But God forbid,
the youthful blood of the saints,
Hector Peterson and Solomon Mahlangu
to be shed in vain

Mr President, preach the intimidating truth that
others never had enough courage to preach.
We want to be converted
and to be baptized in the rivers
of a socio-economic free South Africa.
We don't want a president of any political party,
burn all political organizations
on the altar of the people's emancipation.

No nation can rise above the integrity of its leaders
and no matter how hard a leader can strive for
higher deals

the efforts are futile if he dines in Jezebel's table.
Reshuffle the system.

We want a President of the people.
One who will listen to our cries, echo our voice
and bear our stripes of pain.
The history of this nation insists.

We want a President of the people.
A cabinet the youth can relate to;
with a sense of mission that is commanded by the
people.

A President who is so sold out to his people,
he cannot be bought by any silver nor gold
that he would rather choose to die
than to live in a dream that betrays his people.

A President that would rather choose to die
than to serve his stomach
and enter the Promised Land alone
while leaving his own people eating crumbs
of false freedom behind.

The Vir[in]us

Some said it came from the East,
some said it profited the West.
Some said drink *uMhlonyane*,
some said there is no vaccine.
The analysist said the masses are misled.
The masses said the analysts are confused.

Some said it's in the air,
some said it's in the mind.
Some said it's in the churches,
some said it's in the taverns.
The poor said it came with the arrogant rich.
The rich said it came with the negligent poor.

They told us not to panic, the state is prepared;
but when it finally came, they dug masses of graves.
Some cursed the media for spreading the fear,
some cursed the politicians
for worshiping the greed.

They told us we need the IMF bank
to maximize resources
but when the relief package of billions came,
they enriched their own pockets.
Some said it's worse than HIV and AIDS,
some said it's 666: The mark of the beast itself.

Some said it's the survival of the fittest,
some said it's the vengeance of God's judgement.
Some said it's time to adjust to the new normal,

some said the new dawn of the New World Order.

The social media wokist said
stay away from the damn vaccine.
The social media preacher said
Lord protect us from the doom that's coming.

Fires of My Hometown

This place has known fires.
The hell fire,
the arms fire
the fire of dreams,
the fire of fame
the fire of Rastafarians,
the fire of Pentecostals
this place has known fires.
Crown, surface, and ground fires
all fires, including the fire that burns inside you.
Hammarsdale has known fires.

From 1983 to 1992 Hammarsdale was burning,
the fires of two opposing political views.
The fires of social disaster like Chernobyl fumes.
The fires of Daluxolo Luthuli,
the fires of Zakhele Nkehli.
The fires of UDF, the fires of IFP.
The streets became living hell,
Schools caught in the cross fire of bullets,
perishing souls, metal pipes, and gunpowder.
Breast milk in the ring of fire,
some were born into it, some were born for it
and some were born against it.
The fire of peacemakers,
Eternal homages and gratitude to Sipho Mlaba
and Meshack Hadebe,
Forever to be remembered.

This place has known fires...

The fires of greed, the fires of wrath,
the fires of vengeance.
The fires on the streets, routes and township ranks.
The fires of comrades,
rebels and political bloodshed.
Is it about who has the best hitman?
or who burns the strongest incense?
It's dog eats dog,
flesh eats bones
It's survival of the fittest,
It's survival of the heartless
manufacturing widows, orphans,
and shattered homes.
The fires of Can's wrath,
the fires of Abel's blood.
Fear is the worst fuel of the fires.

This place has known fires...

The fires of the ghetto
Will either ignite your passion
or reduce your dreams into carbon ashes.
Some say the township is toxic
and some say the township is prolific.
Some are ashamed of where they come from
and some are proud of where they come from.
Words can be your passport
if you have the ambition to soar high.
The fire of the pen may not erase your yesterday
but it can rewrite your future.
Ode to those who set the fire on global stages.
The fires of Gcina Mhlophe,
the fires of Fred Khumalo.

The fires of Writers, Poets and Story tellers.

This place has known fires...

The pitch fires of our Soccer stars
MacBeth Sibaya and the fire of the national squad.
Sbusiso "Rhee" Zuma was a foot fire-juggler on the
pitch and a launcher of fireballs on the net.
Remember the brilliance of Boy-Boy Mosia?
gone but not forgotten; a tragic supernova.

Hammarsdale has known fires.
The fire of soul, Thembisile Ntaka
gave us "Save Me"
that soulful hymn you breathed sister never gets old.
That fire of drama Pearl Thusi
unleashed on"Queen Sono"
and burnt it down like Alicia on the piano,
This girl is on fire.

This place has known fires…

The fires of mob justice.
The fire that torched Bheki Nzama
and his reign of terror.
Burn the system for social negligence,
burning questions about the raging fire
of Gender Based Violence.
Sulfuric acid tears burn my eyes,
gully erosion on my cheeks
as I recall recent victims.

In the heart of these streets
sometimes justice is a hobo.

Gunshots wounds in her chest and head.
Kidnapped and found dead,
her name was Noluthando Khomo.
The heart of this place was ripped out on broad day,
the day Snegugu Linda's body was found
disembowelled and dumped on a pathway.
Not long before that Nomvuselelo Ngcobo went
missing and her family was still in search
when in the same area, a burnt woman's body
was found dumped in a ditch.

Zinhle Xulu was shot and killed
in front of her family
but the killer got out on R2000 bail;
a disgusting mockery.
My heart bleeds, I'm heart burned.
Justice for Sbahle Ndlela
raped and strangled to death by her stepfather.
Rekindle the fire of justice.
Rekindle the fire of the people's conscience.
Burn the silence. Burn the indifference.
Burn the fear. Unleash the fire.

This place has known fires…

These skies have been adorned
by exquisite pyrotechnics
you should see the fireworks in Hammarsdale
on the 31st of December, the vibe is pandemonic.
The fires of *shisanyama*, chicken dusts
and township flava.
The fire of peri-peri sauce on fried chips
and for extra bucks you can add some hotwings.
The grill, the sports fever and Sunday chillas

49

and the fire of *imbawula* on winter shivers.
Hustlers on these streets selling Mo'Faya
striving black businesses, Kasi empires.
If you're politically well connected,
you can score some tenders.

This place has known fires...

Fires of prayer, this place is Jerusalem.
Fires of brimstone, this place is Gomorrah.
Flames of the zodiac twins,
one thirsts for righteousness, one addicted to sin.
Hammarsdale is a tale of the civil war within.
This place has seen the blazes of darkness,
and the flames of faith that revives the hopeless.
These streets have seen the cycles of fire;
the fires of burning tires and barbed wire,
the fires of redemption songs and Bob Marley.
The fires of tongues and tent revivals
from preachers;
the fires of the Phoenix that rose from the ashes,
the fires of Vulcan the counterpart of Hephaestus.

This place has known fires.
The hell fire,
the arms fire.
The fire of dreams,
the fire of fame.
The fire of Rastafarians,
the fire of Pentecostals.
This place has known fires.
Crown, surface, and ground fires
all fires, including the fire that burns inside you.
Hammarsdale has known fires.

Blood Nation

"Stabbed and hacked [cut repeatedly into pieces in a rough and violent way, often without aiming exactly] with an axe."(06/06/2020) Her name was Naledi Phangindawo, 25.

"Pregnant, stabbed and hanged on a tree." (08/06/2020) Her name was Tshegofatso Pule, 28.

Even without any graphic images the mere reading of these headlines make one's mind bleed. It would have been daring enough to say someone must imagine these stories as some fiction but now it's even more mentally heavy when you have to process it as a projection of reality. While we are still trying to deal with the pandemic of Covid-19, another pandemic of femicide is still going strong here in South Africa.

Some say the "red" colour on the Brownell's design of the South African national flag represents the "blood" which was shed during the struggle for liberation. It was meant to be a remembrance. Today, that "red" might as well represent the blood of our mothers, sisters and daughters in this Land that is constantly being shed! And it's a haunting reality they have to walk and live in every day. All the women who are brave enough to still go to work and walk in these streets might as well be given a national medal of courage. But how so? If being at home or around the people who are supposed to protect them is also not an assurance of safety?

The Women who hashtagged 'AmINext?' During the awareness campaign of Uyinene's murder never knew they'd answer with their own lives. Bishop Tutu coined the term "Rainbow Nation" with hope to impart a vision on post-apartheid South Africa but it seems like a utopia too far. The present reality is "Blood Nation". It is the current lived experience by women in this nation. There's a new ongoing Apart-heid in South Africa, the one that is not of race but a separateness of human conscience. All men, myself included should be feeling immense shame to live in a society where women are being denied by those of our gender, the intrinsic right and freedom to exist. This existence should entail the dignity, respect, honour and protection.

In the same way Floyd couldn't breathe as the knee of an oppressive system pressed upon him on the streets, Pule also couldn't breathe as she hung on that tree. In the same way it is not enough for a white man to say "I don't see colour" without employing resistance and a decisive anti-racist attitude against all forms of racism. It is also not enough for any man striving to be good and honourable in our society to say "I'll never hit/abuse my woman" without a strong resistance against the prevailing atmosphere of gender based violence against women. There needs to be a strong 'antiness' to speak resistance in our circles as men and to protest, emotionally and physically in this ongoing socio-gender struggle.

It's ignominious that while we support international protests of 'BlackLivesMatter' yet right here at home in S.A, women and children are screaming in our backgrounds. This cannot be a normal we accept. May God deeply stir our hearts to act on this burden and revolt against this social curse upon this Nation. May God help us!

The New Bro Code

Zab Lamena is my friend and an environmental
activist at heart. I reminisce about our final semester
at varsity when we were staying together at res.
Every time when we went to the shops to purchase
some groceries, Zab would call me out and confront
me for buying plastics. I really thought the dude was
being melodramatic, trying to be Captain Planet on
me.

I would feel the strong protest in his voice but to
me, buying plastics was my habit but to him, it was
a bad habit and he made it a big deal! Every single
time, without fail he'd constantly remind me not just
as a friend but as a fellow conservator not to
contribute to the already hazardous plastic waste.
Suffocating our environment; plastic waste can take
up to 450 years to decompose; some studies say up
to 1000 years. Polluting our oceans; environmental
scientists predict that by 2050 the mass of plastics in
the oceans will outstrip the mass of all fish that lives
there. Consequently, it is also predicted that by 2050
every species of seabird will be accidentally
consuming plastic debris.

I didn't take it seriously at first but every time his
words would marinate in my mind. Eventually I was
baptized with the same environmental conviction
and my habits started to reform, I now use durable
shopper bags instead. Besides, it's also green for the
pocket. You see, Zab couldn't save the entire world

but he began the conversation within his circle. With me, he revolutionized the way I think about plastic.

On gender based violence (GBV), if we gents can employ the same mentality, attitude and zeal, we can change the narrative. But we also have to possess some level of deep conviction that GBV is utterly wicked and evil and that nothing would ever justify it. We must also be educated about it so that we may educate one another and challenge it intelligently. In our daily conversations, let's mind the way we talk about women. When someone says something crooked within your space about any woman whether you know her or not, it's not of necessity, what's critically important is that you are there and those perverse words of "entitlement" are landing on your ears, what are you going to do about it?

Be an activist right there! Call out the brother and bring him into order whenever he has a 'trashy' tone about any woman. Make it a big deal! And make sure at departure, your resistance was felt. We must have zero tolerance on anyone in our circles who has even the slightest inclination towards gender based violence. Don't worry about your seeds of resistance; they will contemplate about your words and never undermine the power of impartation. Your little seeds will germinate and behaviours will change.

We can't correct actions if we don't begin first with our daily conversations. Conversations reveal the frame of mentality. Listen attentively, be conscious of the words, comments and strive by all means to correct a distorted thinking about any entitlement on women. It starts with me. It starts with you. It starts will all of us as men. Let's begin to return the place of dignity, respect and that intrinsic worth in women that we have stolen as men. It matters not who they are, what matters is that as men we have a moral obligation to shield every woman around us from any potential harm or danger, especially from insecure masculinity.

We must think about them correctly, we must speak about them correctly so that we may also begin to love them correctly. This is one of our parts we could play, it may not seem like much but it is something. We may not save the entire world but we can begin with conversations, we can construct new and better conversations. We can talk, until that talking shapes new behaviours. Protect the woman even when she's not there because she might never have a chance to ever protect herself. We may differ about who's the GOAT between Messi and Ronaldo, we may not see eye to eye on the Soweto Derby, we may argue about the ANC and EFF. That's okay. But when it comes to gender based violence or any hints thereof, we must all be on the same page. On the same paragraph. On the same line of thought. This is imperative. This the new bro code.

Brotherhood

As the sun rises
and collaborates with the sky
to produce a beautiful morning,
a brother is already awake, tying his shoe laces
and ready to secure the meal for the evening.

Life is an everyday hustle
on this side of the street
and survival is an everyday struggle
to make ends meet.
The process in the trenches
is the hardest part of the dream
mad love for these brothers
who keep fighting and never quit.

Half of these brothers
grew up in homes absent of fathers,
but see them grow into men,
becoming true daddies to their own children.
See them feeding the family
and honouring their mothers.

I see young bread winners
who never had the privilege
of luxurious options,
some laboured for minimum wages
and never tasted elite education.

But a brother always has a plan.
What you see today is just an attendant

in a petrol station
but tomorrow that's a high profile client
in a different dimension.

So this right here is dedicated to the brotherhood,
this is where we grind and strive to survive.
This is where we help each other
and build one another
we make mistakes, take the lessons
and correct the wrongs.
We start from bottom
until we make the refined dough.

The brotherhood defines
the chronicles of the street journal.
The brotherhood is the rumble of the hustles.
The brotherhood is the hub of the bread winners.

The movers that move
the tectonics of the concrete jungle,
the shakers that shake until scattered pieces of life
assemble like a magic puzzle.
The brotherhood is the cradle of game changers.
Long live the brothers with a plan,
I salute you street soldiers,
May you find the hustle's paradise in the Land.

Zozibini

To be young, black and gifted.
Oh what a time to be alive!
Haven't you heard?
Sons and daughters of Alkebulan arise!

They tried to sell us a false image
telling us Black is the colour of crime.
But look at the mirror African child and be proud
because Black is now officially the colour of prime!

In 1971, Gill Scott-Heron professed
that the revolution would not be televised.
In 2019, a black and beautiful princess of the soil
gracefully adorned the Mouawad Crown!
These are the turning chapters of history
that will never be forgotten.
A story I will live to tell my sons,
daughters and grandchildren.

So rejoice you dark and lovely child of the soil,
your princesses are no longer in Disney Land
but in the neighbourhood of your skin.
The world has become your stage to own it so
aim for the stars and don't be afraid to put the
galaxy in your pocket!

Speak your mind with confidence and
walk with unapologetic boldness.
Let your melanated presence
be felt by the audience.

Show them the colour of your love,
You are a true descendent of greatness.

Let the African dawn shine on your face,
Let the wise African proverbs
guide you in your path.
When they think you can't handle this prominence,
when they try to turn down your pace,
adjust your crown and tell them you've got this!
In the words of our Miss Universe:
Take up the space!

Black Love

Black brother, brother sister
what we have is each other.
Mama told us to stick together.
No matter the sound of the raging fire,
we can walk through the flames
and conquer together.

Don't let 'em come between us.
Whatever was formed to kill us
will only leave us stronger than ever.
With a love so bold,
we can mend these broken walls
and rebuild our home.

See how our black sisters flourish
when they're loved and honoured by black brothers.
See how our black brothers overcome
the world against the odds
when they're cheered and encouraged to push
forward by black sisters.
We were meant for each other.
No one understands our black pain more than us
and ain't nothing stronger
than that classical black love.

Let's love each other.
Let's rekindle the fire.
If we are the source of each other's pain,
who in this world could ever heal us?

'Cause only a black hand can understand a black wound.
Black brother, black sister
What we have is each other.

A Prayer for Spiritual Discernment

Help us Lord to not only discern evil spirits
and false prophets
but to also discern unheard cries
and shackled voices.
Help us discern rape,
when that girl child who comes to Church
is being molested by her own father.
Help us discern the psychological trauma
of that brother who had no one to talk to
when his right to dignity
was monstrously stripped away from him as a child.

Help us Lord to not only discern false doctrines
but to also discern the orphans in our midst.
Help us to discern the young preacher
who has just preached a powerful sermon
even though he had nothing to eat except
drinking water for the past 5 days when he slept.
Help us to discern the boy
who comes from a destitute family,
the one who matriculated meritoriously
and got accepted at University
but doesn't have money for registration,
 deposit for accommodation
or to even buy the bus ticket.

Help us Lord to not only discern cold worship
but to also discern depression.
Help us discern the suicidal thoughts of that sister,
even though she has a generous smile

and seems to be doing well in life.
Help us discern the hopelessness
that consumes our pastor's mind,
even though he had just concluded
a bible series about faith.

Help us Lord to not only discern
the signs of the end times
but to also discern the signs
of the cold love inside us.
Help us discern our injustice,
indifference and hypocrisy
even though we proclaimed your love
yet failed to exemplify it in practical theology.
Help us discern that church hurt is real and many
couldn't even access a chance to heal;
even though this place was meant to be
an institution of Grace.

Lord help us to not only discern cults
but to also discern needs.
Help us discern empty stomachs.
Help us discern broken homes.
Help us discern drowning souls.
Help us discern where a little gesture of kindness
is needed the most.

Lord help us to not only discern spirits,
But to also discern humanity.
To not only discern eloquence,
but to also discern silence.
To not only discern Satan,
but to also discern You.

Lord help us to discern;
You in those who are hungry.
You in those who are thirsty.
You in those who are strangers.
You in those who need clothes.

You in those who are sick.
You in those who are in prison.
You in those who are alienated from justice.
You in those who are silent victims
of gender based violence.
Lord, help us to discern You.

Part III

When I was a Little Boy

When I was a little boy,
there was no chore that I hated more
than sweeping the yard.
The dust would go up so violently like a sand storm
I could feel it at the passages of my nostrils
and at the back of my throat.
My legs would be covered
with all of its grimy coating.
I would throw the damn broom to the ground
and storm back inside the house.
From the bottom of my heart
I cursed the arid ground for this devastation
and cursed the skies for refusing precipitation.

When I was a little boy,
my aunt would make her own rain and
every time before she swept outside
she would fill up a jar with water,
and she would start sprinkling it on the yard while
humming her favourite song.
She swept like she made art,
she swept like she knew the fairies of the dust.
My curious heart began wondering
how something that gave me so much agony
was able to give her so much peace?

When I was a little boy,
my aunt taught me that if we waited for rain
or dwelt in bitterness,
we would never sweep.

We have a choice to create the rain we want
and it doesn't take a storm,
just enough in a jar to make the soil happy.

"But aunty, why do you enjoy it so much?" I asked
and she told me to be mindful
of the therapeutic earthly smell
that rose every time she sprinkled the soil.
It's one of the most soothing scents
you will ever smell.

If we could learn how to make our own rain,
we would rejoice even in days of draught.
Gratitude turns chaos into order,
It just takes a little tenderness to release the aroma.

Now when my world becomes dry and dusty,
I fill a jar of attitude with what my aunt taught me.
I sprinkle the situation with sweet water.
I sprinkle it with laughter.
I sprinkle it with prayer.
I sprinkle it with love;
until it softens and releases the aroma that I want.

I Believe in Me

My mind is submerging under my ink flow,
my ink flows in the direction
of the channel of thoughts.
Words of life plunge inside my arteries,
words of healing gush
like eternal streams inside of me.
Predestined to birth greatness,
I can feel the labour pains of destiny.

A jar of honey taught me
to revere the Bee's little wings,
so I dream towards greatness
while nurturing these humble seeds.
The aim is not to conquer the altitude
but to fly with purpose
and at all times land in gratitude.

If life is like tertiary education,
Graduating through trials is my portion.
No matter how hard the system
may knock me down,
I will continually rise and refuse to dropout.
Behold the chronicles of a legend unfolding,
I can feel the labour pains of destiny.

To My Love at First Write

It was love at first write,
the moment I first saw you.
I know I stumbled to find
the *write* words a few times
but I'm glad I finally found
the artistic hand to hold you.
I looked beyond your delicate curves
and I saw you for the substance within.
If I told you that you define my purpose of
existence, would you believe me?

You got me up all night, down
and out with these love poems
I'm trying to spark the flame with these *J coals*
and I'm feeling bubbly like Colbie Caillat.
But you give me more than just tingles in my toes,
you're an ever fixed mark in the fabric of my soul.
I'm not a fan of tattoos
but I love the ink in your vain.
What am I going to say
when you make me feel this way?

I remember the first date,
I couldn't afford to take you to the 2 Quire concert
but you were my ride or die Pilot,
so we *jottered* down into a journey of 72 pages.
Before I knew it,
we were making love on the white sheets of paper.
I'm trying not to stray from the margin
but can you remember those first nights

of tight tripod grips… The very first magic?

Enough with the poetic romance,
you're the confidant of my heart
and soul and you know that.
You've always been there to listen
to my inner thoughts.
You're not just a simple pen
but a fine stick of the Writer's tree of life itself.

Some see you as a weapon of war
but I see you as an instrument of love.
Sometimes I wonder, though this is a scary thought;
without you in my life, what would be the point?

Contaminated World

There's a lot of acid rain these days,
a precipitation of corruption and deception.
Civil gangsters that disguise themselves
as civil servants.
Modern slavery that disguises itself
as political liberty.
War that disguises itself as peace.
Infection that disguises itself as a cure.

Pride, greed, hatred and cruelty.
These are the toxic gases suffocating humanity.
It's a harsh environment to raise children,
getting exposed to a plastic world
where people fake emotions
and good deeds are polluted by corrupt motives.

We're confining animals to extinction,
Polar bears and White Rhinos
lament our indifference to the situation.
The destruction of forests is ever more
and whoever tries to be the Lorax
is an enemy of them all.
Don't try to change the norm,
get your gwap and conform to the show.
Confusion and disorder is the ruling order;
the irony about global warming
is that the world is getting colder.

High on Love

Love is a drug you cannot overdose,
stronger than the most addictive substance
but you cannot sniff it through the nose.
You can't swallow it like pills
but you can taste it with the taste buds of your soul.

Love will penetrate the walls of your pericardium
and hit your phrenic nerve
as strong as a heart attack,
It's a feeling you cannot escape.
Let it encapsulate your heart.

Love is the reverse of anaesthesia.
Love compels us to feel.
Whether we feel the heaviness of joy or grief.
Love is the killer of all indifference and
as you love, you are bound to feel.

Love compels us to feel all its shades.
Love commands a state of awareness,
Awakens all our senses
and resurrects whatever corpses of feelings we had
buried inside.
Love is a sobering drug.

In an age of slumbering consciousness
and emotional numbness,
Love is the drug we need.
The coke of all soulfulness.

The Lightbulb to the Ice-Cream

I know you like living in a cold world
and often dark in this cabin called a fridge.
But allow me to be your spark,
your ever present light.

I know it's quite of a weird combination
even when you think about it,
we are fire and ice.
But I'd like to show you
that even the heat that emanates
from the filament of my soul,
will not be a threat
when it seeks to melt your heart.

You bring joy and spread smiles to a lot of faces
and I just want you to experience the warmth
you so beautifully give to others.
I know it's easy for me to say the future is bright
because I define it.
But that sweet flavour of your smile
is the only thing that's missing in my world.

I hope you see the world needs both sparkles of
light and sprinkles of love.
Forgive me if I'm sounding a little bit *coney*
but it is my duty to show you how much
I'm prepared to love you *un-cone-nditionally*.

You see, my motives are clear,
you can see right through me.

So transparent there's nothing to hide.
Naked like a child at birth you see all that I am.
And that bowl shaped vacuum inside of me
only you can occupy.

So here we are under the stars,
Like John Legend sung, heaven is not too far.
Except for you and me;
we both have our weaknesses.

"I'm too delicate," they say.
"You're too tender," so I've heard.
To me it sounds like you and me
were already *mint* to be.

They said if I'd fall for you I'd crash into pieces,
But that's a risk worth taking,
So long as I'm falling into your love.

Let's electrify this moment.
Maybe this is the time,
I'm a man of truth but I definitely wouldn't mind to
be sugar coated by you.

The Greatest Scam

Failure is not necessarily the opposite of success
but sometimes an essential part of it, towards it.
Sometimes success is concealed in failure.
Sometimes the first kiss of success
is just behind the veil of failure
but often we never discover this beauty
because we refuse and fear to see through the veil.

Perhaps we should start seeing failure
a bit differently;
not as an enemy but an ally.
Not as a delayer but as a preparer.

The fear of failure is the greatest scam.
It not only robs us of the possibility of success
but of the definite experience and lifetime lessons
we would have obtained
if we were not so afraid to fail.
It robs us of the wisdom,
perhaps we never would have known,
If we had we succeeded, at first trial.

<u>Gideon</u>

For every battle a Warrior is born.
The greatest discovery in life
is not what you uncover from the crusts of the earth
but what you excavate
within the layers of your soul.
Buried under doubt, fear and insecurities
there is a giant inside
that defines your endless possibilities.
I hope someday you awaken
that mighty Warrior inside of you
or at least encounter a voice that will drill inside
and introduce you to your true self.

Rarity

"Real is rare," the young girl said.
"Not at all," said the old woman,
"Real is actually common but the true sight
to see what's real is rare."

To My Unborn Daughter

One day I'll tell my daughter:
Little girl, listen to Daddy,
there's nothing you can do to make a man stay
and there's nothing you can possibly do
that would justify a reason for him to cheat.

It's not your job to make sure you 'tick'
his imaginary boxes,
It's not your job to conform
to the image of his ideal wife material.
But it's his job to love you for who you are
And not what he thinks you're supposed to be.

My daughter, never ever blame yourself
for a man that cheated on you.
A man's integrity is not a matter of circumstance
but of firm will.
So, never try to look into your flaws
to find answers for why he did it,
for something that is at best a question
of his moral reflection.

You are Art.
Most men will be curious when they meet you
but remember,
It is not your job to satisfy the longing
of their questions
If they have not found their own answers already.

You are Art.

You can't control how they choose to look at you
but you're certainly not for every man
to touch or to handle.
Your colours, your texture
is certainly not for every man to carry.

Be bold because you are already beautiful;
you will never depreciate
because of what they fail to see.

You are far too valuable and precious,
with intrinsic worth.
Because you are my daughter,
a fearfully and wonderfully made piece of art
In God's magnificent gallery of creation.

Friends like Sunshine

May you have friends who will inspire you
to fall in love with life again.
Friends who will remind you
what a beautiful world it is
and what a course of celebration it is to be alive.
How beautiful it is to breathe,
eat, taste, laugh and love.

May you have friends who will make you notice
the beauty of the brightness of the moon at night.
Friends who will send you random pics of breath
taking views of the sunset hues.
Friends who will make you inquisitive about garden
flowers and little creatures.
Friends who will awaken you to the beautiful day
outside despite the ordinarity
And shake you off from what Dawkins called the
"anaesthetic of familiarity".

May you have friends who will make you laugh
and appreciate the weird formations of the clouds
as if they were God's own doodling
when He shows His lazy creative side.
Friends who will teach you
how to dance in the rain like children
and remind you to hold your umbrella upside down
to collect pennies from heaven.
Friends who won't punish you for dreaming.
Friends who'll cultivate your childlike wonder
and ignite your imaginative thinking.

If the world is a cold place;
friendship is the campfire of the soul.
Everybody deserves the soulful nourishment
of laughter and joy.
Life is a road trip best travelled in companionship,
then it becomes an adventure.
Sometimes a day seems like
just any other ordinary day
until a friend awakens you
to the aurora in the horizon.

Part IV

Conversations with Three Sparrows

I woke up this morning
echoes of yesterday's hail
still lingering on my ceiling.
Today I had hoped for Sunshine
but a dark cloudy mood dominated the sky.

Reminds me of the
turbulent storms that have passed
and how I haven't seen
a silver lining in a while.
I rose from my bed with an inverse smile,
tensions of tomorrow already wearing me down.

Three sparrows pitched by my doorstep
with conversations pure and true.
The first sparrow recited these words,
"Why are you cast down, O my soul and why are
you in turmoil within me?
Hope in God and wait expectedly upon Him."
The sparrow told me: "This is my message to you,
the wrestle of emotions you feel inside
is merely the yearning of
your soul for a rock that is higher than yourself.
There is a rock your soul can climb,
a rock of living fountains that banishes all forms
of despair; the Rock of Ages."

The second sparrow recited these words,
"The steadfast love of the Lord never ceases,
His mercies never come to an end;

they are fresh every morning."
The sparrow told me: "This is my message to you,
your mind is too fixed on the noise
that overwhelms you,
that you've utterly missed the wonderful portrait
of the hand that sustains you.
Your very story is a biography of grace.
The title of it is: Unconsumed."

The last sparrow recited these words,
"Do not be anxious about anything; instead.
Pray about everything.
Tell Abba what you need and thank Him
for all He has done."
"See the three of us," said the last sparrow.
"We sow no grains in the fields
or store food in the barns.
None of us can tell you where
or when we'll find the next meal
but we all drank and ate this morning.
I can also assure you sir
that none of us will go to our nests
starving in the evening.
So if we, mere little creatures of the sky
are met so attentively with daily provision
at the point of grace;
How much more you who are made in God's very
own image? Could any of us ever be more valuable
to Him than you?"

I woke up this morning,
echoes of yesterday's hail
still lingering on my ceiling.
Today I had hoped for Sunshine

but a dark cloudy mood dominated the sky.

But all of that ceased to matter right now
because three sparrows pitched by my doorstep
with conversations pure and true,
they reminded me of how tremendously God loves
and takes care of His Creation
and how I'm intrinsically
and genetically valuable to Him.

Then I saw all my troubles evaporating into air,
knowing that every day
I encounter His ever dwelling grace.
Sometimes how I feel may
not align with what is true,
even then, I am treasured. I am loved. I am secure.

Ancient Israelites

So long as the presence of God abided with them
the milk and honey flowed endlessly.
The essence of the milk and honey
never was about the state of the Land but
about their spiritual state with God.

Poetic Sketches of Psalm 23

•"The Lord is my shepherd, I shall not want"
There are things in life we need not pursue,
If we decide to pursue God first.
•The "green pastures" are not defined by colour
but by the presence of the Shepherd.
•Do not drain yourself in labour, take time to rest.
God is not a fan of weariness hence
"the still waters".
•No pastures, no matter how green they may seem
are worth it at the expense of your peace.
•If God did according
to my sinful deeds I would be doomed
but because He does according
to His name's sake, I am blessed.
•Faith is not about denying
the reality of darkness in the valley
but trusting God to lead you through
the bleak of darkness and depth of the valley.
The antidote of fear is His presence.
•There's comfort in the rod and staff;
a wise soul values genuine
confrontation and correction.
A wise soul treasures the gentle rebukes of the Lord.
•When God prepares you a banquet,
it doesn't matter who disapproves.
He seeks no permission from any
human council to release His blessings.
•When your cup overflows to the brim,
remember to pour into others.

•"The Lord is my shepherd," as you abide and
follow in this pattern;
you become irresistible to goodness and mercy.
They shall also follow you restlessly.

When Fear is Inside the Room

Courage is the conversation we have with ourselves
when the murky presence of fear is inside the room.
We mustn't wait for it to go away
before we speak the truth we've been entrusted with.
We mustn't wait for it to subside
before we embrace the mission
we've been called into.
We keep conversing inside as we press onward;
intensifying the conversation
and encrypting it in the language of faith.
Fear is a lover of subservient silence;
It hates being interrogated,
It hates being questioned.
Don't let it rule inside, converse!

<u>Mellow</u>

I'm a trinity that consists of the spirit,
 body, and soul.
With this light that I hold,
I cultivate the soil and let the flowers grow.
I spark the African dawn
and enlighten the minds of the old,
young and the unborn.

I paint images for the blind.
I compose rhythms for the deaf.
I am the true melody of a Writer's
hopes and dreams.

A pathfinder's journey is not an easy slope,
take this scope with a seed of hope.
In this challenging globe
with God's guidance and His path to follow,
Consider my path mellow.

To Love Mindfully

I think when you're in a relationship with someone
you should be able to look at them
and think to yourself,
"Wow, it really makes perfect sense for me
to be with this person."
I think you should be able to justify with logic,
not just with feelings;
sound reasons for being in a relationship
with that person.
I think a relationship must have
that intellectual element;
to love a person not just with the heart,
but with the mind.

9 Questions

Can you measure the universe?
Can you deplete the ocean?
Can you number the grains of the sand?
You see, God created it all,
now imagine the scale of His love towards you…

Can you travel the distance between the stars?
Can you tame the radiation of the sun?
Can you alter the course of the earth about its axis?
You see, God sustains it all,
now imagine His providence towards you…

Can you change the law of gravity?
Can you suspend the laws of chemistry?
Can you rewrite the laws of motion?
You see, God designed it all,
now imagine the design of His plans towards you…

The universe is complex.
Life itself is an intricate puzzle.
Even the most basic things are held
by finest calculations
and God is the eternal mathematician
who governs it all;
the solver of the most complex
trigonometric equation of Sin.

The God who governs the world
of such overwhelming science
immerses Himself in divine poetry.

Pouring His heart out and writing
with the ink of His own blood;
a love scent of ages…
You are always the subject
of everything He composes.

Makwenzeka

Makwenzeka uphel' amandla endleleni,
Makwenzeka kuphel' ithemba inhliziyweni,
Makwenzeka imimoya yok'phila ivunguza,
Makwenzeka is'khathi sobunzima sik'fica,
Makwenzeka abangani bek'shiya,
Makwenzeka izihlobo zik'lahla,
Makwenzeka uhlangana nalenkondlo…

Kuzo zonke izinkondlo engingaziloba,
Umdali ungiphe yona le namuhla.
Mhlawumbe ukuba ngik'khumbuze,
Noma k'ngenzeka konke,
Kodwa yena owuqalile umsebenzi
kweyakho impilo uzakuw'feza.
K'ngenzeka konke,
Kodwa elakhe icebo ngeyakho
impilo alinak'vinjwa.

Uthando lwakhe luphakeme kunoThukela
Lubanzi kunoMngeni
Lujulile kunoMfolozi.
Kuyoqhekeka izintaba,
Kuyobhidlika amadwala,
Kuyowa isibhakabhaka nezinkanyezi
Kuhlangane impumalanga nentshonalanga
Kodwa olwakhe uthando lumile nawe njalo.

Likuqhuba endleleni,
Likwembathisa amandla amasha,
Likuthwala ebunzimeni,

Likunika ithemba elisha.
Uthandiwe! Uthandiwe! Uthandiwe!

Thatha lenkondlo uyilobe enhliziyweni,
uyivalele ngophawu lothando.
Makwenzaka ukhohlwa,
uyivule kuwe ngaphakathi.
Makwenzeka nomunye eyidinga,
Uyihaye ngelakho ilizwi.

If it Happens (A translated poem of "Makwenzeka")

If it happens that you grow weary along the way,
If it happens that hope decays in the heart,
If it happens that the tempest of life rages,
If it happens that a time of despair
tumbles upon you,
If it happens that friends forsake you,
If it happens that family abandons you,
If it happens that you come across this poem…

Out of all poems I could possibly write,
God gave me this particular piece today.
Perhaps for me to remind you
that even if the worst may befall,
He who began a good work within you will fulfil it.
Tragic things may occur
but His ultimate design for your life shall never fail.

His love is higher than uThukela,
Deeper than uMngeni
and wider than uMfolozi.
The mountains shall crack,
the hills will collapse,
the sky and stars shall fall,
the east and west horizons shall clash together
but His love shall always stand, unshakably.

His love pilots you on the journey,
It clothes you with rejuvenated strength,
It carries you on the shoulders

through difficult times and
it gives you a new hope for tomorrow.
You are loved! You are loved! You are loved!

Take this poem and write it upon your heart,
seal it with the seal of love.
If it happens that you forget it
just look for it inside you.
If it happens that another soul needs to hear it,
recite it with your own truest voice.

A Portrait of Self-Love

Selfless love is not the opposite of self-love
and self-love is not the same as the love of self.
You should never lose the truth of your being
in the curve of loving someone else.
Authentic love affirms identity,
It doesn't deform nor despise it.

The love of self exalts the self.
Self-love exalts the love itself.
In self-love the self is nurtured,
kept healthy and nourished.
So that when the self is laid down
for the sake of others,
It is laid down or given as a whole
and unified self.

Giving the self that lacks in wholeness,
a self that is deficient of identity
or destroying ourselves in the process of giving
until the self becomes unrecognizable;
deprives us of giving to another person ever again
because we have depleted the actual self to give.

But giving in whole
enables us to give even more.
Self-love does not prevent selfless love,
It makes it meaningful.
So, by selfless love
If a whole, healthy and oxygenated love is implied
then the self must be nurtured

to be enabled to give itself
in the measure of wholeness.
Selfless love is not a love void
of the true essence of self
because whenever selfless love is experienced,
the true self of those that give is revealed
and the true self of those that receive is restored.
In selfless love we give the self, engulfed in love.

Selfless love is not the opposite of self-love.
Tell me, how can you truly give
a whole love to another person
while fracturing your soul
and cutting yourself into pieces?

Part V

Manifestation of Light

So soft I breathe,
in the calmest of my degrees.
I find myself holding the pen like a paint brush
and the paper like a canvas.
Trying to portray the vision that I see,
of a Land not too far from here.
Where there was a nation of all races
but nobody was hungry.
A people from diverse tribes
but nobody was thirsty.

They were filled with love
and fulfilled the duty of love.
They lived in harmony
and shared relationships of integrity
because they were believers and keepers of faith,

They cherished and practised
the values of The Book.
With His words, they sang in devotions
their hearts woven together
by prayers of connected emotions.
Like an onshore breeze,
this is something that felt refreshing to feel.

Knowing that somewhere,
if we could just spark it clearly;
in these streets… In my streets.
In these people… In my people.
Peace can be cultivated.

Hope can be rebuilt.
A true journey can begin
and a manifestation of light can be found
from the place within.

A Mother's Prayer

A mother's prayer is a dedication of the mind
that breathes for a life.
A mother's prayer is a mother's
tremendous love expressed
and a mother's place and care unmatched.

A mother's prayer is a mother's
weapon of love that fights
and protect all her children.
It crashes slithering serpents
and slams cunning forces.

A mother's prayer is deeply
rooted in the hope inside,
constantly seeking all that is best
for her children.
A mother's prayer is like
a walking stick in a mother's journey.

A mother's prayer sings for joy and cries for all.
A mother's prayer is bridge of hope
between the earth and the throne of Grace.
A mother's prayer is a shield and a sword of faith.
A mother's prayer flows naturally
from a mother's heart,
It spreads the fragrance of warmth
and invites God's presence in homes.

We know God hears these prayers,
We know God answers the mother's prayer

because a mother's prayer is selfless
and the very DNA of her children's
bread and basket.

At Calvary

We have found a place like no other;
we have found a shelter beyond all other shelters
where there are no limited spaces for souls
from different walks of life to rest.
Where everybody can drink to quench
his eternal thirst.
Where everybody can find bread to satisfy
his eternal longing.
We have found a place like no other.

We have travelled different places.
We have bowed in different altars that have
demanded sacrifices from us
but here, we have found a place where
a sacrifice was made for us.

The voyages are over,
the searching has ceased.
The wandering is no more,
our hope is sealed.
Sealed eternally in this place.

Forward my new address to the enemy
that's been chasing me!
Our souls have found eternal security.
In this place, no foes can triumph;
a place of liberty.
A place that our souls have been
given rest from all misery.
That's why we sing and shout:

Burdens are lifted at Calvary!

Under a Constructive Fire

Fire can symbolize the end;
the ashes and the smoke.
It can also symbolize a fresh beginning;
the flourishing and the hope.

How many fires have forests endured?
Yet come sprouting season,
new vegetation explores.

Do not cancel yourself under the fire;
some of the tallest trees in the forest
were just little seeds that did well
under the pressure.
You see, some seeds need
to encounter the flame
before they can truly germinate into a growth
 that no one can tame.

Man of Calvary

We have a Saviour who knows the marrow
of our human struggle,
not by virtue of being omniscience
but by walking and breaking bread
in the depth of our experience.
While religions proclaim the omnipotence of God,
in Him we saw the vulnerability of God.

His presence does not mean pain will not be felt,
It means hopelessness will not be
our dwelling place.
We know He can establish our healing,
the only physician of the soul.
He alone never becomes alien to our pain.

Ode to Hope

I can't really pinpoint when our relationship began
but I know that you were there for me
even before I became conscious of your presence.
The earliest memory my mind serves me
was when my mom went away for a business trip
when I was a child.
Lord knows, although she was away
for only three weeks,
to me those were the longest three years of my life.

I'd cry every evening and every time
I heard the front door opening,
I'd hope that this was finally her
arriving back home.
To put it simply, although the exact word
that captures the full weight
and essence of what I was going through
during those days was not yet invented.
I'm definitely sure that what
I was going through then
is what now we've come to know
in South Africa as *"umgowo"*.

Yet something so strong kept me
going during those days.
Something kept a large part of me
more eager to wake up in the morning;
I had the strong anticipation that my mom
would walk through that door someday
and it was you, oh Hope it was you

who kept me going.
My heart leaped like a puppy when your tender
whispers were fulfilled on one evening
and indeed my mother walked through the door.
Hope, it was your hand
that ushered me to the castle of joy.

Reflecting back;
perhaps that was some divine setup.
Some sort of blind date,
me being the blind one of course;
for us to intimately know one another.
Maybe God's wisdom saw
that since in a few years down the line,
death would crawl and undermine
the *storge* bond I had with my mother,
It would be the ever constant *agape* bond
that would constantly be my shelter.

Fast forward the time,
when I grew into a man
and began to realize how wretched the world is
and how little it really has to offer.
It became clear to me that I had to take our
relationship more seriously and more intentionally.
You were the reason I believed there's something
better than this grim world
and the tender strength that kept me going through
my own internal battles as well.
Hope, it was you who gave me some sense
when everything was senseless.
Hope, it was you who was my point of reference
when everything else seemed pointless.

Through Christ, a matrimonial kiss was sealed.
In Him you became even more personified;
a mystery unveiled.
Even though a matrimony has inherent limitations;
that's why spouses utter, "till death do us apart."
But in our union, death shall not have the final say
because even if the time comes
before the sounding of that final trumpet,
even in death, as I rest,
you Hope shall be my pillow.

Come resurrection morning,
where the skies shall be adorned
by the constellation of Angels.
In the twinkling of an eye,
my eyes shall behold the infinite radiance of the Son
and as I ascend to meet my Saviour,
I shall wave goodbye.

I know you shall be smiling
because everything you had whispered
would now be finally fulfilled
and everything I had hoped for
would now be finally revealed.
I shall never forget you through eternal ages
I shall be thankful
because I never would have made it
to the Celestial City without you.

In 2014, I had a very bright and lovely classmate by the name of Pinky Mbeje. She was a very kind person with big dreams and she was honestly one of the most academic competent learners in class but shockingly she passed away in that year while she was on the edge of finishing her matriculation, she never got the chance to write her final exams. Now this was my first realization, awareness and clarity of the absence of any claims I can make about being more deserving than others to receive this gift of life.

Fast forward to 2020, a lot of things happened in that year that made me remember and appreciate the truth of the closing poem of this book which is titled, "To live is Grace". That thought settled deeply on my mind on one Sabbath morning and I was inspired to write this poem. This is perhaps my love poem to you, to remind you that life is precious than gold. I am truly grateful that you dedicated your time to receive these poems and I hope something also germinated inside you. May we live conscious of this truth; to live is Grace.

To live is Grace

At any point in your life, climax or low.
At any point in your life, whether rich or poor
may you never forget this simple,
honest yet highest truth: To live is grace.

To live is grace means that
there's nothing we can possibly do
to earn any right for tomorrow.
No matter how noble your thoughts may be,
they do not guarantee you the precious right to live.
Yes, even in your purest journey
like embarking to church,
spontaneous disaster may still find its way.
Like a sniper, carefully coordinating your moments
before taking everything away.
There's no secure license of living
to escape the cunning ways of death.

Because life according to death,
means that every breath taken
is an opportunity for calamity.
But when mercy says "No"
It matters not the accuracy
of the target on your head,
death can still miss and that is why
To live is grace.

Look, death is not an amateur.
It is as old and experienced as sin.
Death is not a respecter of age;

the old citizen dies but so does the infant
at some tragedy, even the promising youth.

Death is not a respecter of the status of your wealth;
the poorest of the poor die
but so does the filthiest of the rich,
at some tragedy, even those who were
yet to taste the fruit of success.

Death is not a respecter of family union;
the father dies but so does the mother,
at some tragedy, even the children.
Death is not a respecter of race;
the black person dies but so does the white,
at some tragedy even heroic
figures of humanity on either side.

Like the wise preacher,
one might be tempted to question
the purpose and sanity of it all.
As you analyse the subject
you might label everything "vanity of vanities!"
but do not be quick to drift away,
as I wrote this poem I began to ponder
about how the paper that I wrote on
was an element of a dead tree.
Until the pen that I held poured life on it
in the form of ink
so that the words I recite from it
are the words that breathe.

No matter how hard the reality of death,
the fact that you and I are still recipients of grace
does not make us better people,

but it challenges us to live better.
To honour the opportunity
and celebrate with excellence
the luxury of possibilities.
It gives life meaning,
perhaps more distinct
for you and I to discover
why we were given this day to live.

Honour small moments
with the fullest of your presence.
Love all persons with the purest of your love.
Mind the colour of your words
and paint every verbal picture with significance.
Be true to your Maker,
treasure His word as the most
valuable possession of the soul.

Whatever may befall, in this gift of life
above all, do not forget to live gratefully.
Do not forget to be thankful.
Do not forget… To live is Grace.

Acknowledgements

There are truly many people that cultivated my love for writing and nourished the seed that has germinated into this book. My sister Thobile, introduced me to Hype Magazine when I was doing grade 8 in 2010. This magazine was the domain of hip-hop knowledge and culture in South Africa and I was always captivated by the architecture of words and how its writers were able to draw vivid collages on my brain. My cousin Philani Ntombela, was a madly gifted writer himself and an impeccable hip-hop MC. He's the one who taught me how to think like a writer and helped me refine the coarse surface of my craft and to strive in becoming a better writer. Sometimes we would stay up all night just writing rap songs and poems until the sun shone in the morning.

The germination of any seed depends on certain environmental factors and conditions. I recognize the fact that there's a shed of sunlight and precipitation I've absorbed from different wonderful people that God intentionally placed in my journey. In some contour or texture I've been inspired by many. I've always held a firm belief that God doesn't channel our lives according to places we have to see but according to the people we have to meet. It is those people to whom I also express gratitude.

Special thanks to Sandisa Phungula for the exquisite and narrative illustrations he contributed to this work. True gratitude to Zolile Machi, the creative editor of Gcwala Magazine for being part of the crucial process that saw the true germination of this seed. Endless gratitude to Clement Sibanda for the tremendous patience and tenacity that truly advanced this work. True appreciation to Ndo The Poet for gracing this book with such a wonderful entrance through the fragrance of her words. Deepest gratitude to Noxolo Sojola for the premium level of precision she dedicated towards the final refinery process of this work. Lastly, heartfelt appreciation to all the friends and people that believed and inspired the poet in me and the possibility of this beautiful landmark in the landscape of art.

About the Author

Sizwe S. Sithole is a writer and a poet who hails from Mpumalanga Township in Hammarsdale. He studied Nature Conservation at Mangosuthu University of Technology (MUT) and is currently pursuing his post graduate studies in Conservation. In 2018 and 2019 he was awarded the certificate for the best undergraduate speaker of the Ecosystems Rehabilitation and Restoration (ERR) Annual Congress at MUT. As a poet, he was inspired very early by great writers such as Lebo Mashile, Angifi Dladla, Gcina Mhlophe and Sarah Kay. And by the rise of Christian spoken word through Jon Jorgenson, Jefferson Bethke, Clayton Jennings and Janette…ikz. He has performed his poetry at Luthayi High School and Mpumalanga Library poetry sessions.

He has also shared some of his writings and poetry on his Facebook page @ **Sizwe S. Sithole**. As a poet, he has also participated on the Poetry Africa Open Mic competition, the Fundza poetry and Avbob poetry competitions. Through his poetry he elevates the banner of Christ, inspires hope, celebrates black excellence, interrogates the status quo and contributes to the values that uphold the social fabric of society, bringing necessary change.

All these themes are gracefully mingled together in his debut poetry book, The Germination.

About the Illustrator

Sandisa has been doodling and scribbling for as long as he can remember. He grew up watching a lot of anime and reading comic books of all sorts. Drawing his favourite characters from anything and everything he saw. It wasn't long until he started creating original characters that he eventually wrote fascinating stories for (yup, he is a writer too). He later broadened his horizons by getting into abstract art and working as a freelance artist. Follow more of his work @ superflysebentin (Instagram, Facebook and Twitter). mailto:sandisa6620@gmail.com

About the Book

The Germination is what happens
when a mind is soaked in purpose,
when a seed of thought is nurtured
and the writer awakens to the reality of his gift
to strengthen what fear had loosened.

Much of the poems in this collection
were written during the devastating times
of the pandemic,
where darkness seemed to subdue
but courage was needed.

The Germination touches on themes of
Grief.
Hope.
Social justice.
Reluctant dreams.
The colour of love
and the triumph of faith.

Ultimately, the Germination is all about
what you need to personally discover
as you uncover beneath these poems your own seeds
that should germinate inside you.
This book was written
To break the shell of dormant seeds.

www.ingramcontent.com/pod-product-compliance
Lightning Source LLC
Chambersburg PA
CBHW020548030426
42337CB00013B/1007